Collins

easy lea

English

Ages 8–10

Tom asked, "Please may I have a piece of cake?"

Shareen Wilkinson

How to use this book

This book is for parents who want to work with their child at home to support and practise what is happening at school.

Tips

- Your child should work in a quiet, comfortable place, away from distractions.

- Help with reading the instructions where necessary and ensure your child understands what to do.

- Tackle one topic at a time and give your child opportunities to practise.

- Help your child compose sentences orally before writing them.

- Encourage your child to check his/her answers.

- Discuss with your child what he/she has learnt.

- Discuss favourite activities.

- Reward your child with lots of praise and encouragement.

Parents' notes

At the bottom of each page you will find a footnote. **Supporting your child** explains how you can help your child practise the activity. **Taking it further** suggests additional activities and encourages discussion about what your child has learnt.

The vocabulary that your child should know and use by the end of this book includes:

adverbial	*direct speech	*inverted commas (or speech marks)
*prefix	pronoun	*subordinate clause

*This is key vocabulary from *Easy Learning English 7–9*, so that your child can revisit and practise the terms.

ACKNOWLEDGEMENTS

The author and publisher are grateful to the copyright holders for permission to use quoted materials and images.

p.4 © owatta/Shutterstock.com; p.20 © 2008 Jupiterimages Corporation; p.23 © Iriskana/Shutterstock.com; p.34 © pavalena/Shutterstock.com; p.35 © zzveillust/Shutterstock.com; p.36 *Spider McDrew and the Egyptians*, HarperCollins*Publishers* © 2007 Alan Durant and Philip Hopman

Every effort has been made to trace copyright holders and obtain their permission for the use of copyright material. The author and publisher will gladly receive information enabling them to rectify any error or omission in subsequent editions. All facts are correct at time of going to press.

Published by Collins
An imprint of HarperCollins*Publishers*
1 London Bridge Street
London SE1 9GF

© HarperCollins*Publishers* Limited 2014
ISBN 9780007559879

First published 2014

10 9 8 7 6 5 4 3 2 1

All rights reserved. No part of this publication may be reproduced, stored in a retrieval system, or transmitted, in any form or by any means, electronic, mechanical, photocopying, recording or otherwise, without the prior permission of Collins.

British Library Cataloguing in Publication Data.

A CIP record of this book is available from the British Library.

Publishing Manager: Rebecca Skinner
Author: Shareen Wilkinson
Commissioning and series editor: Charlotte Christensen
Project editor and manager: Tracey Cowell

Cover design: Susi Martin and Paul Oates
Inside concept design: Lodestone Publishing Limited and Paul Oates
Text design and layout: Q2A Media Services Pvt. Ltd
Artwork: Rachel Annie Bridgen, Q2A Media Services
Production: Robert Smith
Printed and bound by Printing Express Limited, Hong Kong

MIX
Paper from responsible source
FSC www.fsc.org FSC® C007454

This book is produced from independently certified FSC™ paper to ensure responsible forest management.

For more information visit:
www.harpercollins.co.uk/green

Contents

Prefixes	4
Suffixes	6
Spelling strategies	8
Double consonants	10
Greek and Latin	12
Words from other countries	14
ei, eigh and ey	16
Homophones	18
Apostrophes	20
Standard English	22
Adverbials	24
Pronouns	26
Word classes	28
Direct speech	30
Clauses	32
Paragraphs – non-fiction	34
Paragraphs – fiction	36
Using a dictionary	38
Proofreading your work	40
Myths and metaphors	42
Reading non-fiction	44
Reading poetry	46
Answers	48

Prefixes

Prefixes are groups of letters added to the beginning of words to change their meaning. Examples include **sub–**, **anti–** and **auto–**.

anti– means against

- Write anti– in front of these words. Then cover each word and write it in full.

  anti septic _____

  anti clockwise _____

  anti social _____

  anti freeze _____

  anti body _____

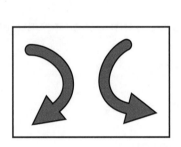

- Check the meaning of each word in a dictionary.

sub– means under

- Write sub– in front of these words.

  _____heading   _____marine

  _____divide   _____merge

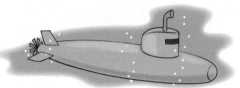

- Look again at each word and say it out loud. Then cover it above and in the Word column of the table, and write it in full in the space provided.

Word	Cover and write	Check spelling
subheading		
subdivide		
submarine		
submerge		

- Check you have spelt the words correctly.
- Now check the meaning of each word in a dictionary.

Supporting your child Encourage your child to use a dictionary to look up the meanings of other words beginning with the prefixes **anti–**, **sub–** and **auto–**.

auto– means self

- Write auto– in front of these words.
- Then cover each word and write it in full.

_____biography _____

_____mate _____

_____graph _____

_____mobile _____

- Check the meaning of each word in a dictionary.

Matching up

- Draw a line to join each word with its meaning.

Word

autobiography

autograph

automate

automobile

Meaning

a handwritten signature, especially of a famous person

to operate something using machines instead of people

a car

a story of a person's life written by them

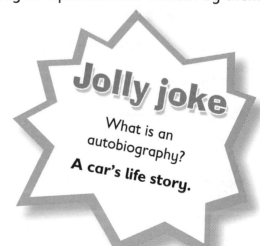

Jolly joke

What is an autobiography?

A car's life story.

Taking it further Encourage your child to use the prefixes **sub–**, **anti–** and **auto–** in their writing, where relevant.

Suffixes

Suffixes are groups of letters added to the end of words.
The suffix **–ly** can be added to an adjective (describing word) to make an adverb.

Example: sad ⟶ sad**ly**

Adverbs can tell us **how** (or in what manner) a person or object does something.

Adding –ly to words

- Add –ly to complete these words.

  quiet_____

  peaceful_____

  calm_____

  comical_____

Changing words ending with –y

If a word ends with y, has a consonant letter before the y and has more than one syllable, then you change the y to i and add the suffix –ly.

Example: happy ⟶ happily

- For each of the words below, change the y to i and then add –ly.
- Write each word in full in the space provided.

  angry ⟶ _____

  lazy ⟶ _____

  ready ⟶ _____

  heavy ⟶ _____

  hungry ⟶ _____

Supporting your child   Help your child to learn how to spell words that end with **–ly**.

Changing words ending with –le

If a word ends with –le, the –le is changed to –ly.

Example: simple ——————➤ **simply**

- Change these words by replacing –le with –ly.
- Write each word in full in the space provided.

gentle ——————➤ _____

humble ——————➤ _____

noble ——————➤ _____

horrible ——————➤ _____

Changing words ending with –ic

If a word ends with –ic, the –ic is followed by –ally (not –ly).
The word public**ly** is an exception to this rule!

Example: basic ——————➤ **basically**

- Add –ally to these words.
- Write each word in full in the space provided.

frantic ——————➤ _____

dramatic ——————➤ _____

romantic ——————➤ _____

angelic ——————➤ _____

artistic ——————➤ _____

Jolly joke

Why are frogs so happy?
They eat whatever bugs them.

Taking it further   Create a poster that shares rules about how to add **–ly** to the end of words. Use the rules given on these pages to help you.

Spelling strategies

Breaking words into **syllables** can help you to remember how to spell them. Every syllable must have a vowel (a, e, i, o, u).

Examples: garden = gar-den   (two syllables)

pyramid = py-ra-mid   (three syllables)

The letter **y** can act as a vowel sound in words; for example, g**y**m, fl**y** and bab**y**.

Syllables

- Say these words out loud.
- Now draw a line to match each word with its correct number of syllables.

Word	Syllables
favourite	4
extreme	3
thought	2
difficult	1
particular	3

Finding syllables

- Copy each word in the table and then write the number of syllables.

  Remember to say the word slowly before writing it.

Word	Copy and write	Number of syllables
important		
interest		
island		
learn		
length		
library		

Supporting your child   With your child, practise breaking up words (such as objects around the house) into **individual beats** or **syllables** to support accurate spelling.

Root words are smaller words that you can make longer words from. For example, **sign** is a root word, from which **sign**al, **sign**ify and **sign**post can be made.

Hidden roots

- Put a circle around the root word in these longer words. The first one has been done for you.

dis(appear)ance

signature

reviewed

helpfulness

selection

untruthful

Follow the pattern

Knowing the root word can help you to spell longer words.

- Follow the pattern and spell the words. The first one has been done for you.

Root word	–ssion	–ted
permit	permission	permitted
admit		
commit		
submit		
omit		
emit		

Jolly joke

Why did the thief wear blue gloves?

He didn't want to be caught red-handed!

Taking it further Build up a list of root words by adding prefixes and suffixes. For example, help ⟶ **un**help**ful**.

Double consonants

If a word has a short vowel sound (e.g. h**a**ppy), it usually has double consonants before the end of the word. In this example, **a** is the short vowel sound.

If a word has a long vowel sound (e.g. tak**e**), it usually has a single consonant before the end of the word. In this example, **–a–e** is the long vowel sound.

Choose the correct spelling

- Read each sentence aloud and then circle the correct spelling.

  The teacher spent all morning **taping / tapping** the children's drawings to the wall.

  A branch kept **taping / tapping** against the window.

  It was pasta for **diner / dinner**.

  The **diner / dinner** enjoyed his meal and paid his bill.

  At Christmas, **holy / holly** is used as a decoration.

  A church is a **holy / holly** place.

Root words

- Fill in the missing root words that these longer words came from. This will help you to work out the spelling rules!
- Write the spelling rules in the table.

Root word	Longer word	Spelling rule
tape	taping	Long vowel, remove the last e
tap	tapping	Short vowel, double the last consonant
	hoping	
	hopping	

Supporting your child   Help your child to understand the rules for adding **–ing**, for words with long and short vowel sounds.

Tinny or tiny?

- Write **n** or **nn** in all these words. Remember: is the vowel sound long or short?

It was a lovely su_____y day in Ju_____e. The sun had

been shi_____ing all morning and Mr Penny was getting quite

ta_____ed as he pru_____ed the gooseberry bush.

He hummed a fu_____y little tu_____e and smiled as he

noticed the ti_____y berries begi_____ing to grow.

Last year his gooseberries had made delicious wi_____e,

and he was a first prize wi_____er in the

Garden Produce Show.

- Now read the story aloud.

Jolly joke

What do you get when you bake a cake in a pan?

Pancakes!

Baking or backing?

If the last consonant is k, you follow the same spelling rule, but instead of writing kk you write ck.

- Look at each picture.
- Then circle the correct word in the label.

backing / baking the car

no **parking / packing**

a poisonous **snack / snake**

Taking it further Make a list of 20 words where having one consonant or double consonants before the ending of a word changes its meaning, e.g. fury boots or furry boots.

Greek and Latin

Word origins are interesting! These two pages give you clues about which words come from Greek or Latin roots.

The ancient Greeks had a different alphabet from us. Their **f** sound is spelt as **ph** and their **k** sound is spelt as **ch** in English. So any words with **ph** and **ch** probably originate from Greek roots.

ph as in telephone

● Write the words for the objects in these pictures, and check their meanings in a dictionary.

_____   _____   _____

ch as in echo

● Write a word for each picture and check the words' meanings in a dictionary.

_____   _____   _____

Supporting your child   Help your child to identify everyday words from other languages to provide clues for spelling.

Other words in the English language come from Latin, the language of the ancient Roman Empire.

You can find Latin roots in words that we use for **one, two, three.**

unicycle

bicycle

tricycle

uni–	means one
bi–	means two
tri–	means three

Jolly joke

How do you start a flea race?

Flea-two-one-GO!

One, two, three

- Fill in the explanations for these words.

A unicycle has one _____.

A unicorn has one _____.

A bicycle has two _____.

You look through binoculars with two _____.

A tricycle has three _____.

A tripod has three _____.

A triangle has three _____.

Taking it further   Look in an advanced dictionary to find the origins of more Greek and Latin words. For example, what does 'rhododendron' mean and which language does 'television' come from?

Words from other countries

In a dictionary, after the word listing, there will sometimes be a word or some letters in brackets, e.g. (Gr) Greek or (Ind) Indian, telling you where the word comes from.

Knowing where words come from can help us to spell them if we become aware of their spelling patterns.

Words from Italy, France and India

 Italy

Many **Italian** words we use are to do with food:

macaroni   lasagna   spaghetti   pizza

Other Italian words you may know are:

piano   umbrella   graffiti   motto

- Look at the spelling patterns, like the **gn** in lasagna.
- Cover each Italian word and write it out below.

_____   _____   _____

_____   _____   _____

 France

We use some **French** words in our everyday lives:

boutique   café   metre   centimetre

- Can you think of any more? Write them here.

_____   _____   _____

_____   _____

 India

In Victorian times, **India** was part of the British Empire.

- Here are some words with different spelling patterns for you to learn:

di**ngh**y   **pyj**amas   jo**dhp**urs

Supporting your child Explain to your child that the English language is constantly changing and that we borrow words from many countries. How many foreign words can he/she find on objects at home?

Word meanings

in-struc-tion
mal-func-tion

- Use a dictionary or the Internet to look up the following words.
  Find out their meaning and which country they came from.

Word	Meaning	Where it came from
bungalow		
restaurant		
kayak		
robot		
anorak		

New words

Below are some words that are quite recent additions to our language. Many of them come from new inventions.

skateboard   Internet   selfie   yuppie   microwave

Jolly joke

How do trees get on the Internet?

They have to log in!

- Look in a dictionary to find out their meaning if you are not sure.
- Can you find any more? Write them below.

_____

_____

_____

_____

_____

Taking it further   Look out for words from other countries when you are shopping. Many shops and supermarkets have goods from other countries. Read the name of the product and try to guess where it came from.

ei, eigh and ey

The long vowel sound **ai** (as in r**ai**n) can be spelt as **ei**, **eigh** or **ey**.

Examples:

Th**ey** made a delicious cake.

My n**eigh**bour is very friendly.

Choosing ei, eigh and ey words

- Circle the words that contain the long vowel sounds ei, eigh or ey.
  Make sure you check the spellings!

vein   day   cake   weight   eight   they   reign   famous

play   train   neighbour   rate   obey   prey   eighth

Sorting ei, eigh and ey words

- Write the ei, eigh and ey words you identified above in the correct box.

ei words	eigh words	ey words

Supporting your child Encourage your child to say words with the long vowel sound **ai** out loud, so that they can hear the sound. Remind your child that the letter **a** can also make the **ai** sound, e.g. f**a**mous, **a**gent, etc.

- Draw a line to match each word with its meaning.

Word	Meaning
weight	person who lives next door or nearby
eight	a pronoun
neighbour	how heavy something is
they	the number 8

Jolly joke

Why did the banana go to the doctor?

It was not peeling well.

Write your own sentences

- Now write a sentence for each of the words.

weight

_____

eight

_____

neighbour

_____

they

_____

Taking it further Ask your child to use a dictionary to look up the words containing the **ei**, **eigh** and **ey** sounds on page 16. Some words have the **ei**, **eigh** or **ey** spelling but are said in a different way, for example height. Your child will have to learn them.

Homophones

Homophones are words with the same sound but different spellings and meanings. ('Homophone' comes from Greek roots and means 'same sound'.)

Often you have to stop and think which spelling is right for your meaning – or check in a dictionary.

Homophone examples

- Fill in the rest of this table.

Word	Meaning
to	before a verb (e.g. to go)
	a number
	as well/also
there	a word describing a place
	belonging to them
	short for 'they are'

Which spelling?

- In each sentence, cross out the incorrect spelling.

I had to **write** / **right** a thank-you letter.

There is a **break** / **brake** on my bike.

It's **grate** / **great** to see you!

Please have a **peace** / **piece** of cake.

Our shorts tie at the **waste** / **waist**.

Which / **Witch** DVD do you like best?

Supporting your child   Encourage your child to use a dictionary when he/she is unsure of the correct spelling/meaning of a homophone.

Which or witch?

The words below are all tricky pairs of words that sound the same but mean different things.

- Check the words in a dictionary. Then write a sentence for each one to show its meaning.

which _____

witch _____

wait _____

weight _____

waste _____

waist _____

Jolly joke

What happens if you see identical witches?

You can't tell which witch is which!

Tricky vowels

- Check the words below in a dictionary. Then write a sentence for each one to show its meaning.

peace _____

piece _____

break _____

brake _____

great _____

grate _____

Taking it further Often, homophones are different word classes (or parts of speech); for example, **write** is a verb and **right** is an adjective. How about **passed** and **past**? Whenever your child needs to spell homophones he/she isn't sure about, it may help if he/she works out what word class each one is. Find out more about word classes on page 28.

Apostrophes

Apostrophes for possession are used to show that something belongs to a person or object.

| the dog's bone | the cat's tail | the car's tyres |

- Rewrite these phrases using apostrophes.

the stripes of the zebra _____

the neck of the giraffe _____

the broom of the zookeeper _____

Plural owners

If there is more than one owner, the apostrophe goes after the s.

| the zebras' stripes | the giraffes' necks |

- Rewrite these phrases using apostrophes. Check how many owners there are!

the bones of the dogs _____

the spots of the ladybirds _____

the spots of the ladybird _____

Supporting your child Check that your child understands the rules for adding possessive apostrophes. Also note that if a proper noun ends in **s**, an extra **s** is usually added after the apostrophe; for example, Jame**s's** bag, Barbado**s's** population.

No apostrophes for plural nouns!

You can only use apostrophes for possession, never for plural nouns.

● Put a tick or cross to show which of these are right or wrong.

The queen's ☐ cat's ☐ were yowling in the yard.

We had burger's ☐ and chips ☐ at Ian's ☐ party.

The farmer's ☐ potatoes ☐ were stored in sack's ☐ .

Hundred's ☐ of people were at the ship's ☐ launch.

Jolly joke

What part of English are boxers good at?

Punch-uation!

Apostrophes for contraction

Apostrophes are also used to show where letters have been taken out and the two words are joined together. This is called contraction.

● Complete this table.

Short form	Long form	Letters taken out
haven't		
	does not	
couldn't		
would've		
	did not	
	might have	
	I have	
we'll		
you're		
	it is	

Taking it further Look out for apostrophes in adverts. Ask your child to say whether they are for possession or for missing letters. Are they in the right place? You can often spot errors in handwritten and printed signs and menus.

Standard English

It is important to be able to write using **Standard English**.

Subject	Present tense	Past tense
I	I am	I was
She	She is	She was
We	We are	We were

Verb tenses

- Complete this table by filling in the correct verb tense.

Subject	Present	Past
I	I do	
He		He played
You	You run	

Verb tenses – right or wrong?

- Put a tick or cross to show which of these verb tenses are right or wrong.

we were	☐		we was	☐
I did	☐		I done	☐
I runned	☐		I ran	☐
we did	☐		we done	☐
he gave	☐		he gived	☐

Supporting your child Encourage your child to read his/her written work out loud to help identify verb tense errors.

Verb tenses in sentences – right or wrong?

- Read the sentences out loud.
- Tick the sentence that uses the correct verb tense.

We was making a cake for the school fair. ☐

We were making a cake for the school fair. ☐

I did my homework last night. ☐

I done my homework last night. ☐

They was happy with the car. ☐

They were happy with the car. ☐

You did a good job! ☐

You done a good job! ☐

Jolly joke

Why did the pupil throw his watch out of the school window?
He wanted to see time fly.

Correcting sentences

- Read the sentences out loud.
- Rewrite them using Standard English.

My friend gived me a present for my birthday.

_____

We was so happy to see the film.

_____

What we done was a secret!

_____

I runned a marathon last week.

_____

Taking it further Play a word game with your child where you say a sentence using the wrong verb tense (e.g. I done it!) and he/she repeats it back in Standard English (I did it!).

Adverbials

Adverbials are words or phrases that tell us **how** (manner), **when** (time) or **where** (place) something has happened.

How? ——→ **Very slowly**, the woman opened the door.

When? ——→ **Later that day**, the boy found his favourite book.

Where? ——→ **In the house**, the people were eating dinner.

Adverbials can also begin with **prepositions**; for example, **where, at, then, before, after**.

Spot the adverbials

- Underline the adverbial within these sentences.
  The first one has been done for you.

<u>When I got home,</u> I made a drink.

Before the shop opened, I carefully counted all of the money.

I ran quickly for the bus yesterday morning.

Last night, I stayed up really late.

The birds ate some berries in the garden.

Supporting your child Discuss with your child how using adverbials can make sentences more varied and therefore his/her writing more interesting.

When an **adverbial** is at the front of a sentence, you often write a **comma** (,) after it.

Examples:

The boy played with his toy car yesterday evening.

Yesterday evening, the boy played with his toy car.

The dog hid behind the tree this morning.

This morning, the dog hid behind the tree.

Jolly joke

Why couldn't the car play football?

It only had one boot.

Using commas

- Rewrite each sentence, adding a comma after the adverbial.
  The first one has been done for you.

As soon as he woke up David opened his birthday presents.

<u>As soon as he woke up, David opened his birthday presents</u>.

Very sensibly the family walked across the street.

_____

Later that evening Sarah made a delicious cake.

_____

During the day the children played in the garden.

_____

Taking it further Play a word game with your child where you say a sentence with an adverbial at the start and he/she says where the comma should go.

Pronouns

Pronouns are sometimes used instead of nouns to avoid repeating the noun in a sentence.

Example: The cat chased the cat's tail. ⟶ The cat chased **its** tail.

The word **cat** is a noun. It has been replaced by the pronoun **its** to avoid repeating the word cat in the sentence.

Pronouns – right or wrong?

- Tick the pronouns.

I ☐   under ☐   my ☐   you ☐   behind ☐

me ☐   beside ☐   she ☐   them ☐   on ☐

Finding pronouns

Remember, the pronoun 'I' is always written with a capital letter.

- Underline the pronoun(s) in each sentence. Use the words in the box to help you.

| he | it | his | I | me | you |

I watched a film.

Are you waiting for me?

The computer made an awful noise when it was turned off.

The man drove his car today because he wanted to get to work on time.

Supporting your child   Remind your child how using pronouns in sentences will make his/her writing flow better. Help your child to understand that words like **my**, **your**, **his**, **her** and **their** are a type of pronoun called a possessive pronoun. They show who owns or is connected to an item (for example, **my** coat, **his** bike).

Fill the gaps

● Choose the correct pronoun to complete each sentence. You may use a pronoun more than once.

his	her	he	them

The girl played with _____ football.

The father held _____ baby.

The boy fell over and hurt _____ leg.

Penny got home from school and put her bag in _____ room.

As soon as _____ came home, the man had something to eat.

The children thought the teacher was unfair giving _____ so much homework.

Correcting sentences

Jolly joke

Can you name two pronouns?

Who, me?

● Rewrite these sentences in the spaces provided. Replace the underlined words with one of the pronouns below.

they	we	it

Katy and I were hungry so <u>Katy and I</u> went out for lunch.

_____

The football team trained really hard because <u>the football team</u> wanted to win.

_____

The boat crashed into the rocks before <u>the boat</u> sank.

_____

Taking it further Ask your child to create his/her own sentences using pronouns. Check that he/she has replaced the nouns correctly.

Word classes

Words have different jobs within a sentence. **Nouns, adjectives, adverbs, pronouns** and **verbs** are all examples of word classes (or parts of speech).

noun   adverb   verb

Faisal carefully watched the beautiful birds so he could take pictures.

adjective   pronoun

Identifying word classes

- Draw lines to match each word with its meaning. Use the example above to help you.

Word	Meaning
noun	a doing or being word
adverb	a describing word
pronoun	describes how, when or where something has happened
adjective	replaces a noun
verb	person, place or object

Supporting your child   Remind your child why it is important for him/her to know the correct grammatical terminology (so that he/she can use word classes correctly when discussing his/her writing and reading).

Fill the boxes

- Write the correct word classes below.
  Use the word classes in the box to help you.

| noun | adjective | verb | adverb | pronoun |

Shireen silently read her exciting book while her mother mowed the lawn.

Jolly joke

What is the most mathematical part of speech?

The add verb.

Write your own sentences

- Now write your own sentences using the word classes below.
- Underline and identify the word classes in each sentence.

Example: Word classes: noun, verb   The dog [noun] jumped [verb].

Word classes: noun, verb

_____

Word classes: verb, adjective

_____

Word classes: adverb, pronoun

_____

Taking it further When reading a book, discuss the word classes being used by the author. Use a dictionary to look up the meaning of other word classes such as prepositions, conjunctions and determiners.

Direct speech

Inverted commas (or speech marks) are used to show when people are speaking. This is called **direct speech**. We always start direct speech with a capital letter.

Simon declared, "I will be ready in 5 minutes!"

A comma is inserted before the inverted commas.

Punctuation marks are put inside the inverted commas.

Inverted commas

- Rewrite the sentences below, adding inverted commas (or speech marks). Make sure the final punctuation (! . ,) is inside the inverted commas.

How do you know? replied Sam.

_____

I left my bag at home, exclaimed Hardeep.

_____

Would you like some help? asked the shop assistant.

_____

How? asked Rob.

_____

Adding commas to direct speech

- Put the comma in the correct place to complete these sentences.

Josh shouted "I'm not ready yet!"

Susan replied "I am very well, thank you."

Mark whispered "Please be quiet!"

Supporting your child To help practise writing direct speech, say some sentences out loud and ask your child to write them down using inverted commas (e.g. Mum asked, "Please can you lay the table for supper?")

Using other words (**synonyms**) for **said** will help to make your writing more interesting.

Examples: whispered shouted exclaimed pleaded asked stated replied

Writing interesting direct speech

- Change the words in the speech bubbles to direct speech.
  Try to use some of the words above.

_____

_____

Jolly joke

Why did the pupil take a ladder to school?

She was going to high school!

Taking it further Look carefully at how direct speech is used in books. Remind your child that it takes lots of practice to get the punctuation right in direct speech.

Clauses

A **clause** is a part of a sentence and has a subject and a verb. It can be a **main clause** (which makes sense on its own) or a **subordinate clause** (which gives extra information within a sentence and uses conjunctions like **while**, **after**, **although**, **when**, **before** and **because**).

main clause → | subordinate clause →

Katie looked behind her | because she heard a noise.

subject ↑ verb ↑ | subject ↑ verb ↑

Subject and verb

- Underline the subject in red and the verb in blue in these simple sentences. The first one has been done for you.

  <u>I</u> <u>made</u> a cake.

  She plays football.

  They watched the talent show.

  He cooked some breakfast.

Find the main clause

- Underline the main clause in these sentences. The first one has been done for you.

  <u>I made a cake</u> because I was hungry.

  She plays football when the weather is warm.

  They watched the talent show before visiting their friends.

  He cooked some breakfast because he was hungry.

Supporting your child   Help your child understand that the subject of a sentence can be a **proper noun** (for example, **Katie**) or a **pronoun** (for example, **we** or **it**).

Find the subordinate clause

- Underline the subordinate clause in these sentences.
  The first one has been done for you.

  She went to the bank <u>because she had no money left</u>.

  Although I was tired, I finished my homework.

  I read my book while relaxing on the beach.

  When she arrives I will let you know!

Jolly joke

Did you hear about the riot in the library?

Someone found dynamite in the dictionary!

Write your own sentences

- Write three sentences with a subordinate clause.
  Use the words below to help you.

while	after	although	when	because

_____

_____

_____

_____

Taking it further Remind your child that using main and subordinate clauses in his/her writing will make it more interesting.

Paragraphs – non-fiction

In **non-fiction** texts, you need to organise your writing around a theme or a particular topic. **Subheadings** help you to organise your writing into paragraphs and explain what each paragraph is about.

Comprehension

- Read the comprehension text about the ancient Egyptians.

The ancient Egyptians

Seven thousand years ago, people in Egypt lived on the banks of the Nile – the world's longest river. The river flooded every year, leaving behind black mud and silt (a type of clay). The people living by the river called themselves 'People of the Black Land'.

Subheading

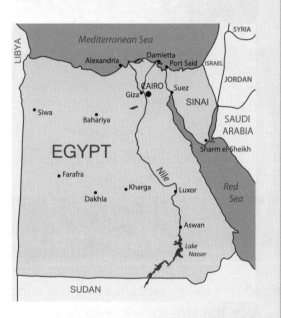

Mummified bodies

The people of ancient Egypt believed in an 'afterlife', which was a heavenly place where people living a 'good life' went after their death. One of the requirements of being able to enjoy an afterlife was to have a preserved body. They preserved bodies by 'mummification' (turning them into a mummy).

Look at the second paragraph and answer these questions.

1. What is the subheading? Write it below.

_____

2. What is the paragraph about?

_____

_____

Supporting your child   Read a range of non-fiction texts with your child and encourage him/her to read independently.

Ancient Egyptians' tombs
There were different types of burial. Poor people were buried in simple graves in the sand, while rich and important people were buried in small tombs. The most important people, the pharaohs (Egyptian kings), were buried in pyramids, which were very large stone tombs. In the centre of a pyramid was a burial chamber. It held the mummified body of a pharaoh. Items were placed in the pyramid for the pharaoh to use in his afterlife – jewellery, clothes, food and drink.

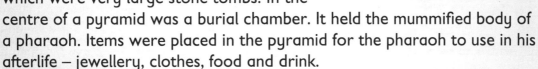

1. Underline the subheading in this paragraph.

2. Now circle the two pronouns that are used to avoid repeating a noun. Write them below.

_____

Writing subheadings

Jolly joke

Why is the pharaoh boastful?

He sphinx he's the best!

- Read both paragraphs. Add the correct subheading above each paragraph.
  (An archaeologist is someone who studies the past.)

Tutankhamun's tomb	Valley of the Kings

The Valley of Kings is called this because it is where the Egyptian kings were buried. Before 1922, 61 tombs had been discovered in the Valley of the Kings by archaeologists. The tombs (built 1539–1069 BCE) were very different from the pyramids and had been kept hidden by being carved high up in the rock face.	A wooden box was discovered buried in the Valley of the Kings in 1907. Written on the box in hieroglyphs (ancient Egyptian writing) was the name 'Tutankhamun', who was known to be an Egyptian pharaoh who ruled over 5000 years ago.

Taking it further When you are reading non-fiction books, focus on the use of subheadings and how text is organised into paragraphs. Discuss what works well and whether you think the page layout could be improved further for ease of reading.

Paragraphs – fiction

Paragraphs help you to organise your work.

You can start a paragraph with a **topic sentence** that tells you the **topic** of your paragraph. The rest of the paragraph should have **supporting details** that explain the topic sentence.

Spider McDrew

- Read this comprehension text about a boy called Spider McDrew.

Spider McDrew was a hopeless case. Everyone said so – his mum, the teachers at Parkfield School, the other children in his class. They said it when they looked at him with his sprouty hair like the leaves of a spider plant (that's why his nickname was Spider). They said it when he had clothes on all inside out and back to front ... and they said it when he got things wrong. He got things wrong a lot because he tended to carry on thinking about something after everyone else had stopped, so he was often one step behind.

Spider's class was learning about the Romans. They had looked at books about the Romans and coloured in maps of the Roman Empire. Soon they were going to dress up in Roman costumes and do a school assembly. To prepare for it, their teacher, Mr Smithers, was taking them on a day trip to the museum.

"Has anyone been before?" he asked the class. A few children put up their hands.

"Please sir, I went to see the mummies, sir," Darren Kelly said breathlessly. "They was wicked."

"*Were* wicked, Darren," Mr Smithers corrected him.

"Yes, sir, they was," Darren confirmed.

"Mummies had their brains pulled out through their noses," Neil Phillips added happily.

Topic sentence – this tells you what the paragraph is going to be about.

Pronouns are used to avoid repeating the noun every time.

Ending sentence

A new paragraph can start with **direct speech.**

In a conversation, there is a new line each time there is a different speaker.

Supporting your child   Remind your child that you start a new paragraph when you change the topic. A new topic could include change of time, a different person speaking, a new character or a new event.

Use the text on page 36 to answer the following questions.

1. Look at the second paragraph. Underline the topic sentence. Write the sentence in the space below.

_____

2. What is the second paragraph about?

_____

3. Circle five pronouns that are used to avoid repeating a noun. Write them below.

_____

4. Look at the last paragraph. Why is the direct speech from each speaker written on a separate line? Use the information in the margin to help you.

_____

Writing a paragraph

Jolly joke

Why did the picture go to jail?

It was framed!

● Use the topic sentence below to write about what Spider saw when he got to the museum. Use the picture to help you. Remember to use lots of adjectives and adverbs.

Spider slowly entered the huge museum.

_____

_____

_____

_____

Taking it further When reading fiction together, identify and discuss the topic sentences. Alternatively, cover a topic sentence and ask your child to use the supporting details in the paragraph to guess what the topic sentence could be.

Using a dictionary

Using a dictionary is vital – to check spellings and to build vocabulary. Sometimes you need to use the first three or four letters of a word to help order them.

Alphabetical order

Dictionaries list words in alphabetical order.

● Write these words in alphabetical order.

| guide | group | grammar | guard | grown |

_____

_____

_____

_____

_____

Features of dictionaries

● Draw a line to match each feature below to the correct entry in this dictionary extract.

headword

word class (part of speech)

other forms, e.g. plural

definition

example sentence

bored
ADJECTIVE When you are **bored**, you feel tired and impatient because you have nothing interesting to do.
boredom NOUN
boring
ADJECTIVE Something **boring** is so dull that you have no interest in it.
born
VERB When a baby is **born**, it comes out of its mother's body.
borrow borrows, borrowing, borrowed
VERB When you **borrow** something, someone lets you have it for a while but they expect you to give it back later.
boss bosses
NOUN Someone's **boss** is the head of the place where they work.
bossy
ADJECTIVE A **bossy** person likes to tell others what to do.
both
ADJECTIVE OR PRONOUN You use **both** when you are talking about two things or people. *She wanted **both** pairs of jeans.*
bother bothers, bothering, bothered
VERB I If something **bothers** you, it annoys you or makes you feel worried.
VERB 2 If you **bother** about something, you care about it and take trouble over it.
bottle bottles
noun A **bottle** is a container for keeping liquids in. Bottles are usually made of glass or plastic.

Supporting your child Make sure that your child has access to a dictionary at the right level for him/her.

What do these mean?

- Look up these words in a dictionary and write down the meanings.

navigate _____

reflect _____

planet _____

constellation _____

plough _____

Jolly joke

Which chocolate bar lives in outer space?

The Milky Way!

Which would you use?

- When would you use each of these words? You might need to look up their meaning in a dictionary!

glossary _____

dictionary _____

thesaurus _____

index _____

contents list _____

Taking it further Each time your child is unsure of spellings or exact meanings, encourage them to look up the word in a dictionary. Does your child use a spellchecker or an online dictionary to check their spellings? How does it compare with a hard copy dictionary?

Proofreading your work

There are several things to think about when writing.

1   While you are writing, think about what you are trying to say.

2   When you have finished, read your writing aloud to see if it makes sense. Check the punctuation to see if the message comes over clearly.

3   Check the spelling. Highlight any words you are not sure about. Look them up in a dictionary or use a spellchecker.

4   Show your work to a friend, as it can be easier to spot someone else's mistakes.

Check your spelling

- Do these words look right to you?
  Check their spellings and write any corrections.

  notice _____

  because _____

  easyly _____

  barly _____

  holyday _____

  polite _____

Supporting your child   Encourage your child to read through his/her written work carefully to check for errors in meaning, punctuation and spelling. Remember, it is easy to correct errors and improve work if you are writing on-screen.

- Read this newspaper advert and correct the spelling and punctuation errors.

CAKE CRISIS – SHOCK HORROR!

All readers will know Mr jones newtowns popular baker. Mr Jones has a problem he hasent got enyone to mind his shop when he gose on holiday nexed week. if he doesent find someone there will be no bred or cakes on sale all week if you wood like to take over mr jones's shop plees right to him at 11 High street, newtown.

Jolly joke

What occurs once in a minute, twice in a moment, but never in a day?

The letter M!

Beat the spellchecker

Sometimes a computer's spellchecker won't catch an error, because the word is spelt correctly but used with the wrong meaning.

- Correct these sentences. Then rewrite them in the space provided.

They said their were no more buns. _____

Hear they come, as fast as they can. _____

My mother said she was write as rain. _____

Taking it further Look out for misspellings in newspapers, signs and menus. Despite proofreaders and spellcheckers, some errors still creep through!

Myths and metaphors

Greek myths are stories that have been passed down to us from the ancient Greeks, who lived about 2500 years ago. Greek myths have had a lot of influence on our familiar stories. Their use of **similes** and **metaphors** has also influenced our use of poetic language.

Characters from myths

The characters in Greek myths were often gods who had come to live on Earth. Here are descriptions of three characters from a well-known Greek myth.

Echo: a nymph, which means a goddess of nature. She talked too much, and so was made to stop talking. From then on she could only repeat things other people said, which is why we use the word 'echo' to mean a repeated sound.

Narcissus: the boyfriend of Echo. He was very vain, which is how we get the word 'narcissist', meaning a vain person.

Hera: the goddess of women and marriage. She was the person who cast the spell on Echo. This was because Echo tried to trick her by talking too much so that Hera could not find her husband, who was hiding from her.

Greek myths

- Use a dictionary to find the meanings of these different kinds of ancient stories.

Legend _____

Fable _____

Myth _____

Supporting your child   Read Greek myths with your child and discuss the different characters.

Similes and metaphors

A simile is when we compare something to something else.

Echo talked so much that it was like a river rushing on and never stopping.

A metaphor is when we say something is something else.

Echo's talking was a river in full flow, rushing on and never stopping.

- Write a simile and then a metaphor to describe Narcissus's vanity (see page 42).

Simile

_____

_____

Metaphor

_____

_____

Jolly joke

What do clouds wear under their clothes?

Thunderwear!

Tell the story

- On a separate sheet of paper, try writing your own story about Echo and Narcissus.

  Use similes and metaphors to describe your main characters.

  Think about why Hera cast the spell on Echo.

  How do you think Narcissus reacted when Echo could only repeat what he said?

Taking it further Discuss with your child what influence Greek myths have had on the stories we tell each other about people's characteristics.

Reading non-fiction

Although the theme running through pages 42–47 is echoes, the non-fiction text on this page has a very different purpose, a different kind of language and a different illustration style from fiction or poetry.

Why do echoes happen?

Sound is caused by vibration. This could be the vibrations in someone's windpipe when they talk, or the vibrations that happen when two heavy objects hit each other. Every sound has vibrations as its starting point. The vibrations move outwards in waves from the starting point.

Sound waves can travel through air and water. They can even travel through solid things like iron, wood or the ground. They travel out in all directions from the starting point – just like ripples on a pond. If a sound wave reaches your ear, you hear the sound.

Sometimes a sound wave travelling through air or water hits something solid, so that some of the wave bounces back and starts to travel in the opposite direction. If this reflected sound wave reaches your ear, you hear an echo.

Sound waves travel outwards from the starting point just like the ripples that spread out over a pond after you have thrown in a pebble.

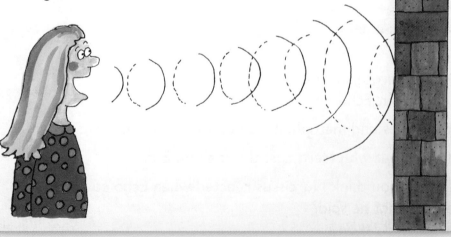

Supporting your child   Remind your child about the differences between fiction and non-fiction texts. Look at some examples at home or in your local library.

Comprehension questions on echoes

- Read the 'Why do echoes happen?' text again. Then answer the questions below.

1. Look at the first paragraph. What causes sound?

_____

2. In what direction does sound travel?

_____

3. Look at the second paragraph. What can sound travel through? Find and copy **three** things.

_____

4. ...*just like ripples on a pond*. Why is this simile an effective way of comparing how sound travels? Use the text to answer the question.

Pctbf

lebgitt2 yourloblox

5. What happens when sound hits something solid?

Pctsimucat ovuPR2hz3

_____

6. What type of non-fiction text is 'Why do echoes happen?' Tick the correct box.

Discussion ☐

Explanation ☐

Instruction ☐

Jolly joke

Why do you always find things in the last place you look?

When you have found it you stop looking!

Taking it further Look at children's books on science. Think about what subjects they are explaining. What kind of language do they use? What 'signposts' do they use in the text, e.g. subheadings, labels and captions?

Reading poetry

'The Horns of Elfland'

- Read this poem to yourself and then read it aloud.

The splendour falls on castle walls
And snowy summits old in story —
The long light shakes across the lakes
And the wild cataract leaps in glory.
Blow, bugle, blow, set the wild echoes flying!
Blow, bugle — answer, echoes,

       dying… dying… dying.

O hark, O hear! how thin and clear,
And thinner, clearer, farther going!
O sweet and far from cliff and scar
The horns of Elfland faintly blowing!
Blow, let us hear the purple glens replying —
Blow, bugle — answer, echoes,

       dying… dying… dying.

Alfred, Lord Tennyson (1809–1892)

Supporting your child   Discuss with your child that this poem is also about echoes. Look at how the style differs from the fiction and non-fiction texts that he/she has looked at in this book.

Explaining the poem

The poem was written more than 100 years ago.

- Find out the meaning of these words.

  splendour _____   summits _____

  cataract _____   bugle _____

  glens _____

- Look at verse one. Which lines rhyme?

  _____ and _____ ; _____ and _____

Jolly joke

What is one of the longest words?

Smile: because it has a mile in it!

Understanding the poem

- The poem is about a boy playing the bugle in the open air.
  Describe the landscape in your own words.

  _____

  _____

- The poet hears echoes of the bugle bouncing back.
  Name four things in the poem that could be returning the echoes.

  _____

- What do you think the poet means by Elfland? Do you think it is real
  or imaginary?

  _____

- How would you describe the mood of the poem? Does it seem happy
  or sad to you? Say why.

  _____

  _____

Taking it further   Read other poems from the nineteenth century. Does your child find the language difficult?
Does he/she learn things that he/she couldn't learn from more modern poetry? Read contemporary poets as well,
and see which you both prefer.

Answers

Pages 4–5

anti– means against
antiseptic, anticlockwise, antisocial, antifreeze, antibody

sub– means under
subheading, subdivide, submarine, submerge
Check your child's spelling.

auto– means self
autobiography, automate, autograph, automobile

Matching up
autobiography – a story of a person's life written by them; autograph – a handwritten signature, especially of a famous person; automate – to operate something using machines instead of people; automobile – a car

Pages 6–7

Adding –ly to words
quietly, peacefully, calmly, comically

Changing words ending with –y
angrily, lazily, readily, heavily, hungrily

Changing words ending with –le
gently, humbly, nobly, horribly

Changing words ending with –ic
frantically, dramatically, romantically, angelically, artistically

Pages 8–9

Syllables
favourite – 3, extreme – 2, thought – 1, difficult – 3, particular – 4

Finding syllables
important = 3, interest = 3, island = 2, learn = 1, length = 1, library = 3

Hidden roots

signature, reviewed, helpfulness, selection, untruthful

Follow the pattern
admission, admitted; commission, committed; submission, submitted; omission, omitted; emission, emitted

Pages 10–11

Choose the correct spelling
Correct spellings: taping, tapping, dinner, diner, holly, holy

Root words
hope – long vowel, remove the last e
hop – short vowel, double the last consonant

Tinny or tiny?
sunny, June, shining, tanned, pruned, funny, tune, tiny, beginning, wine, winner

Baking or backing?
backing, parking, snake

Pages 12–13

ph as in telephone
microphone, megaphone, photograph

ch as in echo
echo, school, chemist

Onc, two, three
wheel, horn, wheels, eyes, wheels, legs, angles

Pages 14–15

Words from Italy, France and India
Check your child's spelling.
Possible French words: restaurant, litre, pâté, quiche, déjà vu, cul-de-sac

Word meanings
bungalow – a single storey house, word from India
restaurant – a place where meals are sold and eaten, word from France
kayak – a canoe, formerly made of animal skin, Innuit word (Greenland)
robot – a machine that carries out jobs normally done by humans, word from the former country of Czechoslovakia
anorak – a short weatherproof coat with a hood, Innuit word (Greenland)

New words
Possible answers: landline, jumbrella, netbook, podcast, ringtone, staycation

Pages 16–17

Choosing ei, eigh and ey words
Ring these words: vein, weight, eight, they, reign, neighbour, obey, prey, eighth

Sorting ei, eigh and ey words
ei words: vein, reign
eigh words: weight, eight, neighbour, eighth
ey words: they, obey, prey

Matching up
weight – how heavy something is
eight – the number 8
neighbour – person who lives next door or nearby
they – a pronoun

Write your own sentences
Possible answers: What is your weight?, I got to school at eight o'clock, My neighbour is very friendly, They went to the football match.

Pages 18–19

Homophone examples
two, too, their, they're

Which spelling?
Incorrect spellings: right, break, grate, peace, waste, Witch

Which or witch?
Possible answers:
I was given an apple, which I ate.
The witch rode around on her broomstick.
I had to wait for the bus.
I ate too many cakes so I put on weight.
Try not to waste so much paper.
Her waist was very small so she needed a shorter belt.

Tricky vowels
Possible answers:
There was peace and quiet when the children went to sleep.
She cut everyone a piece of pie.
If you drop the plate on the floor, it will break.
He slowed down by putting on the brake.
I had a great time at the fair.
They burnt some logs in the grate.

Pages 20–21

Apostrophes for possession
the zebra's stripes, the giraffe's neck
the zookeeper's broom

Plural owners
the dogs' bones, the ladybirds' spots, the ladybird's spots

No apostrophes for plural nouns!
The queen's ✔ cat's ✘ were yowling in the yard.
We had burger's ✘ and chips ✔ at Ian's ✔ party.
The farmer's ✔ potatoes ✔ were stored in sack's ✘.
Hundred's ✘ of people were at the ship's ✔ launch.

Apostrophes for contraction

Short form	Long form	Letters taken out
haven't	have not	o
doesn't	does not	o
couldn't	could not	o
would've	would have	ha
didn't	did not	o
might've	might have	ha
I've	I have	ha
we'll	we will/we shall	wi/sha
you're	you are	a
it's	it is	i

Pages 22–23

Verb tenses
I did, He plays, You ran

Verb tenses – right or wrong?
Correctly ticked tenses: we were, I did, I ran, we did, he gave

Verb tenses in sentences – right or wrong?
Correctly ticked sentences:
We were making a cake for the school fair. ✓
I did my homework last night. ✓
They were happy with the car ✓
You did a good job! ✓

Correcting sentences
My friend gave me a present for my birthday.
We were so happy to see the film.
What we did was a secret!
I ran a marathon last week.

Pages 24–25

Spot the adverbials
Correctly underlined: Before the shop opened, yesterday morning, Last night, in the garden

Using commas
Very sensibly, the family walked across the street.
Later that evening, Sarah made a delicious cake.
During the day, the children played in the garden.